RIDGE OF HIGH PRESSURE

MOUTHFEEL PRESS

RIDGE OF HIGH PRESSURE

poems by

ROBIN SCOFIELD

Mouthfeel Press

RIDGE OF HIGH PRESSURE

Mouthfeel Press is an indie press publishing works in English and Spanish by new and established poets. We publish poetry, fiction, and nonfiction. Our print books are available at independent bookstores, online booksellers, or at author's readings.

Cover Design: Carlos Espinoza

Contact Information:
Mouthfeelbooks.com
Info.mouthfeelbooks@gmail.com

ISBN: 978-1-957840-17-8

Library of Congress Number
2 0 2 3 9 3 8 7 0 1

Published in the United States, 2023
First Printing in English
$16

MOUTHFEEL PRESS

CONTENTS

*Thank you, as always, to the Tumblewords Project,
especially to late founder Donna Snyder, for the original inspiration
for so many of these poems.*

*I would also like to thank the San Miguel Writers' Group
for their brilliant critiques that refined these poems
in various drafts.*

*And finally, I dedicate this book to my husband, whose steadfast
faith in me as a poet has kept me going for many seasons now.*

RIDGE OF HIGH PRESSURE

Ridge of High Pressure

MAY

Coyote nicker-snarls at my black dog
and me, dodging up the hill,
her coat same hue as summer's
yellow grasses and the tan rocks
snaked with ochre under a stalled
ridge of high pressure pushing
moisture away, triple digits
and drought in the El Paso desert
as though our eight inches per year
is too much to ask from the rain gods.
The churlish coyote doesn't flinch
away as she will do,
but steps toward us, curling her lip—
burrowing owls dance by the dam,
and sun jowls creep over the mountain—
as we halt in the heat,
having started too late
for it to be cool, while pups
yammer across the arroyo
in the blue lake of their cave,
and it dawns on me why
she's so brazen—
she's not mad from the heat—
we're blocking mother from den.
My dog Winston and I have to turn
our backs on her and hurry
up the path and down,
no way to go but past her
to get away, as in all the legends.
I am afraid the price
for this hike could be high.
I listen for padded paws behind us,
but blood clamps up my ears
like the hard rain that doesn't come
because the ridge of high pressure
won't budge today or tomorrow.

Then I hear nickers as the pups
settle down. I know she's with them,
she's there like lightning.

JUNE

Under another ridge of high pressure,
we walk at dawn in our urban park
where there is a wildness
to which I cannot speak,
for I don't know how to mourn
the two coyote pups I find
dead on the dam
in early June, pelts slit,
too young to know
to beware the easy prey,
how often a fatal trap
the free dog food or cat flesh.
They didn't know how high
a blood-price had to be paid.

Yet another ridge of high pressure
the color of rust,
an upside down kettle,
as the dog and I climb and
descend on the Three Hills
loop trail. Hot windy days
forecast, haboob and
drought endure
unlike a road that fades
into mirage.
Coyote carries on nightly
drinking from the park's sprinklers
and prowling the desert jackrabbits
that nibble the ballfields, fattening up
and slowing down. Easy food
but at a price. Coyote, without
her pups now, scats on the trail
the gray hair and bones of the hare
whose flesh she has torn and eaten.

JULY

It's supposed to be rainy,
but again, a ridge of high pressure
sifts over us, stifling and tall,
the seasonal monsoon cratering off
the yellow and orange mass
on the weather maps, the west
consumed in cartoonish orange flames.
Before dawn we were up
to walk on the ridge of hills,
my dog, nose-keen
to sense the doe and
her twin fawns
in the arroyo, looking for
water in the hollow spots,
the huecos in
the snake-ridden rocks.
Coyote doesn't know
in her softball paradise
that the western forests
groan under the lightness of fire
and that it makes the beauty
of the sunsets unbearable.
And yet she is uneasy.
She knows the price is high.

Coyote Meets the Ravens

A pup, about five months old,
lies dead on the dam
between the three sister hills.
Ravens surround him,
a family of nodding undertakers.
His pelt has been stripped off
his blood-baked backbone,
the whole arc of
his vertebrae visible—
a rusty bridge spanning
white water. The fluffy,
bony tail still curls out.
Dead for several days
and no rebirth,
just recycling
of eyes and innards
till the park clean-up
crew drives by
and shovels the remains
into the back of their truck.
So the ravens call to their kin
to move on to other dead beings,
their life in the desert.

Heat Death of the Universe

Coyote knows
dawn and slips over
the third dam. Time
to feed the young
and settle in while
the sun bakes behind
North Peak of the Franklins.
I know an old jeep trail
you can spend your time
climbing. Mountains
move through eons.
A stone wears
down. Rain takes it
to a sandy riverbed
though the river won't
flow come fall.
It takes time to break it
in fields where crops
know to blossom then
bear. The bee knows
her circle dances.
At maximum entropy,
I cannot tell the story better
than sparrows scattering.

Watching the Weather

At the fringe of the yellow grass
rolls the supermoon, a giant
gourd spilling seed-stars
on a humid twilight,
black-chinned and broad-tailed
hummingbirds chasing one another.

Purple rain sage foreshadowed
dark sky in daylight, not light
sky at night, not shadows and no
stars tonight. Thunder shakes us
awake. Walking rain stayed
off the ground, dark blue
stripes, the swing of it
in the wind, curving
like a javelina's rib cage.

Green volunteers spring up,
and I wonder if they can outstay
summer's drought and cannon through
to flower and seed themselves,
intersecting a bronze-bodied
rufous hummingbird, between
the setting sun, the supermoon.

Stray trees roam the yard
and lunge at the fence,
weedy palo verdes,
seeded by the wind,
rising in the rain,
the scant rain.

Upper Valley Road, Summer Sunrise

The trill of the red-winged blackbird
carries over the green-smelling water
as he calls for his dull brown mate
who will brood away the summer.

They stay in the cottonwoods, willows,
and Tornillo Oaks here by the Río Grande.
They don't flee like the ducks and coyotes
when the river goes dry in winter.

When I reckon the currents together,
I see that months have gone by, gone
with the spring mornings: minty odor
of salvia, spent perfume of Spanish broom.

On the road, we hear the music
of the mockingbird, torn like paper
in the wind, the taste of dust in my
mouth and nose as the wind gusts.

El Río Bravo, home to la garza blanca.
I would like for you to come with me
under the pines and the downy white feathers
that barely touch us as they drift to the ground.

Desert Landscape in Summer Heat

Hummingbirds thrum and buzz,
click and vibrate with the interior heat
of 1,260 heartbeats per minute:
they rise to fall in the suffocating
afternoon, diving at 90 feet per second,
pulling nine g's when they pull up.

Emerald green creosote stands
stiff and spices the season
with the small yellow flowers
birds dive to claim their nectar,
orange ocotillo like candelabra
against insistent violet sky.

Limitless clock, the hummingbird
ticks back and forth and doesn't slow
down in the thick day I cannot
row through. I'm a boat stalled in
the Sargasso Sea, sails limp, kelp
ensnaring it. By the banks,
it smells foul, but no seaweed,
just sawdust sand where
the burrowing owl dances
on sunlit stones, bobbing
like styrofoam on the foamy,
scum-bearing river.

Stunned Heat of the Borderlands

White afternoon muffles
like a wool blanket. If only
I could have bottled up that
bracing April wind. If only
the wind could ring like
a cold white steeple bell.
If only the bell tower
built in the 1600s
were not so far away
over the magical border.
I could walk there,
past the bridge with so
many people perspiring.
We would die of this heat
without shelter. Coyotes
spend daylight in their dens,
offspring of the desert.
If the July monsoon comes,
the arroyos will rage with
white water. The bell from
1659 will toll in the moist air.
Can you hear it
on the other side?

Talismanic Summer Blues

I hate this time of year:
walking before I get any bearings,
before the rascal sun screams over
the sierras. What would I give
for wind and rain and pine trees,
a carpet of needles under my feet
instead of sharp white stones
and a locus of trails that wind
around and don't come to
a conclusion beyond the coyote den.

The day's too hot for anything
but torpor. Desert creatures creep into
shade, but the sun is long in the sky,
the arc of it farther south, temperatures
and oceans rising. Sit under the fan
and contemplate the future generations
who will do without when we are finished
with this decadent age. Thoughts born
of the promise of rain, a broken promise.
Only dust rises up. Tomorrow I'll go by
the river where I won't feel the drought.
I'll see the red-winged blackbird,
the Great Blue Heron on the wing
before dawn if I hurry before the heat
settles in for a long, hot century.

Border Crossings, Border Wall

Who can keep the Great Blue Heron
out of la Sierra de los Mansos?
Who will see that the lynx can cross?
Their dwindling number threatened already
by the headlights of the Border Patrol jeeps
confusing them about night and day.
Who will tell the gray wolf, by the thinly-
flowing Rio Bravo, that she can no longer
cross? Her haunting howl stretches across
the border to send a shiver down your spine
no matter which side of the river you're on.
No one can keep out the ravens and crows.
There are always plenty of fresh dead
by the river, whether man or minnow.
Don't try to swim across the dangerous,
attractive canals. Call up the buzzards
if you dare. They circle on thermals
that rise from both sides of the valley:
calm, serene, surveying the world
for the dead no one else wants.

The Border as Open Wound

You feel otherness wherever you go.
You can ask the alienist your questions.
But identity is never an easy matter.
You can drop a rock in a pond
and watch the circles drift apart.
Skipping the rock takes some
wristwork. Keeping the rock
and polishing it, that's another
matter, lots of work, but worth it.

You were born an other, a changeling
in your birth family, standing apart.
Je est un autre, Rimbaud wrote,
The I is an other, just as it is
for you, a worldly situation.
A swan walking is a clumsy
animal. You are of two worlds
like the waterbird, therefore
of none. You can claim neither
sky nor lake. And there you are,
walking where the river is dry.

Deadly Nightshade

Sacred datura by the path:
large heart-shaped leaves
and the brown seed pods
that prickle and hang
upside down have scattered
their copious cargo
in late summer drought
on a wind without monsoonal
moisture, but the plant prepares
more moonflowers, even so.
Hallucinogenic and toxic,
levels so close
that young people
looking for a trip die
ingesting it.
Having seeded,
the season dry and
over, you would think
it might shrivel up,
but its new blooms are
rolled tight like cigars,
about to explode
with white light.

August Rain Melancholia

Small white feathers
seesaw down from the pines.
The nestlings prick
with new bristly feathers
after the molt of their down.
This generation to the next—
when it's time to fledge—
they'll be ready, rain or not.

They fall and take
flight at the same time
like a new-born idea.
Under the fallen needles,
I find good dirt. I move
them and make a path
in sand. Under the flowering
oleander, the dung beetle doesn't
filter what's good
from what's bad.
He turns it all the same.
He scrabbles away
from me, in case
my shadow is
a danger. Hard to tell
whether to go on a walk,
half the sky sunny and
half dark, half the sky
silent, half muttering.
I stay close to home,
feeling electric.

Broken Hummingbird

In and out of the yard
like a whisper of rain,
shiny green like the oily
leaves of the creosote bush,
big-eyed and fast,
he would die soon
after trying in vain
the trumpet flowers and feeders,
useless to him with his criss-crossed
beak stuck open in a sideways V,
the translucent straw of a tongue that thrust
at the blooms he helicoptered
at the brink of starvation, his slight frame hiding
a motor that runs at 1,260 heartbeats per minute.

My friends, like Job's, had many suggestions.
Get a butterfly net. Call an Avian Wildlife Vet.
Kill him with a rock to give him an easier death.
No doubt he had given out within the hour.
By his feathers, a young one. He must have
smashed into a mirroring window
when the sun struck it just so,
and his fiery nature ignited
a bird made of light, fighting light,
crashing into solid image:
his kind of kin destroying
the self, that always other,
who turned out to be no other.

The Usual Golondrinas

In the shadows underneath mud-daubed
Artcraft Bridge, the usual golondrinas dive
and soar, circle, and pop in and out of their nests
in gray morning suits, swallows' white bellies
flashing in the sun.
                    The cottonwood fuzzes
the long grasses by the river with their purple heads
as the golondrinas go after the gnats and mosquitos,
who also dwell by the river in a cloud
of Brownian motion.
                    If only I could translate
their murmurations, in Spanish or English, the flocks
of swallows or golondrinas in the mondale pines
and fruit trees these people of the big houses have
planted on their flooding acres.
                    Whatever the weather,
dry river or flowing, the swallows remain
as the ducks and cranes do not. The usual golondrinas'
song mixes in with the ocean roar of truck
traffic, which has increased on Artcraft Road
since the new bridge at Santa Teresa.
                    The usual golondrinas dazzle
with their alphabet of acrobatics, their language of sinew.
The usual swallows remind me that mi amigo
Miguel Angel wouldn't believe me that the English
word for the bird was so feo and only two syllables.
They deserve four for the song,
                    He railed and wouldn't destroy
their nests on the white walls of his porch,
in his big house on Country Club Road,
in spite of their mess by the pool, still so angry
about the English word for la golondrina.

Cyclone

The dust devil grabbed a lawn chair
and packed our noses with dust.
Born of heat and heat slammed together,
a ridge of high pressure stalled
in the west gave birth to this cyclone
that cycles through the day's heat,
the outrageous heat that displaces
dogs and evaporates the rain
before it can fall, and then

we dream of rain, raining down
hard and cold, stinging hailstones,
broken branches, and electric wires.
We dream of rain and seek to stain
our parched lips with sunscreen
and a gloss rain gives to stones
while the wind we can't control
moans and drives the rain over
the granite mountains that make
the weather of our city so very
thirsty.

Dry River

The Great Blue Heron stands over the puddle,
reverse sundial, shadow pointed away from water
so as not to scare the Byzantine settlement
of minnows. He plumbs the settled water,
green-blue with algae, wide wishing-well.
The coming haboob doesn't bother him
in his rapture of fishing when he throws
his head back and swallows a flopping fish.
A sacred meal the shade of dull metal,
and the chalice, a sky-colored mud puddle,
seem fitting among the cathedral cottonwoods.

Meanwhile, the seeds of the tornillo oak
whirl like the cosmos, black hole at the center.
They need soaking when the river floods to undo
their tight spiral of a locked-up seed. The dearth
of rain doesn't help and this crazed sandstorm
so late in the year. To my consternation,
the words for rain turn to dust in my mouth.
Though it's dry as dust, dry and drier,
I plant the sunflower seeds and water them,
keeping a constant watch over a rainless sky.

At Faywood Hot Springs, New Mexico

His skin shone white as adamantine
rock that night under the meteors
loaded with minerals and metaphor,
his hair the color of the gypsum sea
east of here near the rocket range.
I craned my neck in my own
alabaster skin, separate
but joined by the hot springs,
shadowed heads above water,
bodies transmuted by refraction
into the lightness of our youth,
erosion-free and buoyant
in the thermal waters among
the revolution of ancient rocks
that fall and fall in the near
perfect, studded, cobalt sky.
They never thud to Earth,
born again of fire while we are
in pools that capture the one
second flash, one brief life
after another as we go on
singing old songs, warmed
by the steam that boils
beneath a thin, jagged crust.

Enlightenment Blues

Lobsang the Tibetan monk says:
Live in the now. It's Nirvana.
A candle going out.

My mother at 88 does live in the now,
but far from enlightenment,
impatient that no time passes.

       Physicists mark up equations for time
       that move backward and forward,
       but the arrow only goes one way
       as we can see for ourselves:

       never does
       the broken cup re-
       arrange itself
       and jump back
       on the table.

My mother doesn't retain
her arrow of time.
She confabulates the yesterdays
she cannot remember.
She remembers to drink Scotch
and to cheat on the crosswords.
Her addictions have the sense
of history that she presently lacks.

When I meditate to an ancient dialect,
I feel time disappear for twenty minutes.

Her life has tumbled together until she thinks
she is forty again and able to walk.
She crumples to the ground and curses
at the EMS who come to pick her up.

Practice, practice, meditation
until the monkey mind stops chattering.

What persists of her Self, besides swearing?
Not the woman advertising executive in the 1950s,
not the boozing, threatening mother of the 1960s,
not the brassy-haired woman proud to shop at Neiman's.

Not this, not that, said the Buddha.

She calls the knell of the clock over and over,
ringing out like a tower.
She has a flash now and then that her children
don't love her as they love their father.

Live in the present, lose yourself,
says the enlightenment coach.

Ah, but she never loses
herself in her eternal now,
it's clear that's key.
My doctor and I speculate
on her disorder. Narcissistic
with venom, I suggest. He smiles
and says it's bipolar II.

Like me.

> Physicists say spacetime may
> spread so thin in the old universe
> that it will dissipate entirely
> unless dark matter pulls it together
> after there's nothing left in time
> or imagination of you and yours,
> not even ashes.

Fishtailing in East Texas

How much your bruises mattered
when you cried, My arm! My arm!
Speech meant your brain had not
spilled out on the pavement between
lake and pine. Eager desert rats,
we left the bike helmets in the truck,
and I neglected to scout the road.
I should have gone ahead of you.
My judgment under pressure
could not have been much
worse: that steep hill, you at six
not used to the handbrake on the new bike.
Off you went, flying out of control.
Brake! Brake! I yelled, as if
I could will you to stop
as the bike flipped over, and so
did you, my child. I bowed
my head in gratitude that you
could speak my reproach.

Grackle Tragedy

I have thought of them as malevolent,
as too many, as dog food thieves—glossy
black, lemon candy-colored eyes, making
too much ruddy-colored bird poop
that splats from pine tops to car roof.

Today, I watched them grieve as parents
the nestling that fell too early and hopped
around the yard till he fell down dead,
and the ants got his eyes first. Helpless,
the parents flapped and squawked
in obvious distress.

This morning they were quiet
after I removed the body. I heard
the mockingbird's eulogy, the mourning
doves keen away, and the finch
passing the peace with his hymns
of the rising sun.

Through the Mesilla Valley to Tumblewords

at 80 mph on I-10
        wheel out of whack

How fear of death confounds me

in my blue Chrysler about
        to be run over by semis

How fear of death confounds me

        I've got to make
the poetry workshop in Mesilla

How fear of death confounds me

        where Donna and Jesús and I
write and read in a circle and write again

How fear of death confounds me

Next day, I have to get
        two brand new tires

How fear of death confounds me

and two new poems wait
        in my old notebook

How fear of death confounds me

rumbling like trucks
        about to go beyond

How fear of death confounds me

the speed limit, like rockets
        into escape velocity

Unfrayed Means and Ends

"If you say something, see something."
a rope and resin sculpture by Alejandro Almanza Pereda

It is not free and knot free, united in rope.
Untie it, free-standing, soaked in resin.
Understanding (ah, if the walls would let
me!) from outside in. But I cannot. Walk
in the woods. Come with me, outside,
desiring in. Betray me, without walls,
without trees, without path, without walks.
Only fiber keeping a shape of both
the inside and the outside, standing
it over and above. String theory needs
a new gravity, but here is light and air.
Re-minds me. Re-members a shape in
the attractive-only force. Resin resonates.
Cavity captivates, and no doorway invites
me in. Untie it. Unite it, I can't wriggle
free and get inside here, notwithstanding.
If it would let me in, on the inside,
my outside nature become a trap, cabin
all window and without window, only
bars made of hemp, fabric twined and
twinned, twisted into rope upstanding,
outstanding and for standing, under-
standing the need not to be tied in knots
or out of nots, the secret bindings
of round strings and a round of strings.
Remark the remarkable. As this is not
a clear view under florescent light

Strings play without touch, and yet
our understanding is a touch. Just
to see, it changes things, strings them
along a wooded path I can see and say.

Isolated Storms in El Paso

The Perseids didn't show but
shone and cannoned around the sun anyway.
Rainclouds piled up like quilts in a closet.
The lamp stayed on during the day
all day the day the flies escaped us.
Lightning broke out of the ionic sky
and rose from the stunned Earth. One hour
of rusted rain didn't bust the drought
but bounced off North Mountain to clear
the air of dust and bugs, not in time
for us to see the meteors which did
not notice our not seeing them.

Ode to the Apple

after Lorca's "Newton"

You were Newton's clue,
red rose of fruit, freckled
with stars, you grew high

from the *Tree of Science*—
swinging with the comets—
until you fell on his head

that night of the pockmarked
full moon, unlike your satin
face, produce of the sun.

You fell as the moon rose.
Skinny young Newton dozed,
about to upset the Earth,

the mother apple cart, and throw
it out of the center of the universe
where falls all dreck and mud,

according to the alchemists.
You are best when held up
high on the branch—

but do you feel a massive pull
from this slight magnet, Earth?
How did Newton figure gravity

as the arc of falling, you perfection
of fruit—crimson skin, crisp insides,
not white, not yellow—dropping

while the moon stays hooked
in the sky, stuck, wheeling
in imperfect ellipse?

Did he taste you
as did Eve when she took
a bite of you from that other

Tree of Knowledge?
As the serpent god advised
before Adam's bruised ribs

had healed or her wounding
began the birth of others.
A small price to pay,

the bigger price yet to come.
With one taste Adam knew
the love he would have

though he had to leave.
Ah, apple of Paradise, of summer
I get no sudden revelation

of knowledge or love
from you, just the taste
of science as I nibble down

to your poison seeds and arc
you through the air so that you sink
into the trash can, an equation

between eye and hand and core.
I still wonder how gravity adds up
though I observe it every day,

including the moon in orbit,
and you still attached to your stem,
spirit of apple, ghost of a thought.

Apartment Complex

Toddlers wander from the door
with the blue wreath as their mamas
do the laundry. Girls in pink lace
and tiaras ride scooters. Boys make
noise for all their lost causes—footballs
and drama. A pause, as the two women
gossip, one unloading on the other.
Who has full attention? Not the children,
not the one listening to another's troubles.
An animal presence of intuition
is an angel of full attention, my black dog,
whose twelve senses are ignited in his nose.
He knows their feelings better than they do.
Beauty, the terror, is full perception
and includes a toothless crone
and her autistic man-child, dying palms,
and stickaburrs instead of balm in the courtyard.
On puncture vine, a pretty yellow flower persists
before the goathead thorn drops in time
to pierce the bare feet of the children.

Pulling Puncture Vine, *Tribulus terrestris*

Goatheads, poison but not fatal,
you wound a little, hurt a lot.
You are death to bicycle tires
and pierce the dog's paws.
You are not native to the Americas,
but to North Africa and the Mediterranean,
brought by horses' hooves,
the caballos of the conquistadores,
one more plague they spread.
Damnable vines, you seed yourselves
in the thousands and live for a century
underground. I pulled you up
last year in the rain. Last night
it rained a good soaking rain.
Hundreds of you this morning,
devils. I will get you this time
before you bloom and form thorns,
your seeds that travel
continent to continent.
Weather-god, keep raining,
don't let that ridge of high pressure
push the rain away, for after
teaching today there are hundreds
more, it seems. I moved
rocks to get at the tender roots,
white with a bulb of dirt
at one end, a dicot with two bisected
first leaves. So successful at reproducing,
invader species, I will get you
next time it rains before
you spread and flower
yellow, then to make thorns,

first green, then dry grass-colored,
hard and shaped like a goat's head
with two dire horns.
Goathead seedlings,
less than one-quarter inch high,
without weapon except your
succulent white stem, you have
managed to wound me,
poisonous to my bare skin,
thumb and forefinger
sore the next day.
When the monsoonal flow
comes back, I will come
after you again with my leather gloves,
for thousands more of you will sprout.

Haiku of Scorching Heat

Sizzle, bird who hums,
light on the feeder that's yours,
yet you are wary.

No rain, not many
mosquitoes, native
plants need water now.

Blue damselfly, sky
fallen, try to rise, symbol
of impermanence.

The universe dark.
My teacup empty. Water
boiling. Potential.

Hummingbird nest like
a sail and mast sways and dips.
Doesn't break in storm.

Thunder, wind, and light,
Leucophyllum Frutescens
blooms, as with dry tongue.

Dawn temperature
at 80, too hot to rise,
searing to think of.

To My Husband as I Near My 54ᵗʰ Birthday

How time goes like an owl on silent wings.
While I'm surprised to find that I'm not young,
Thirty years with you have passed like a wink.
You are the one who truly knows my tongue.

I've a glimpse of age, then my youth again.
Darkness falls over the mountain, eroded.
I make sure you and I have heard the wind,
What the canyon verse I produce has boded.

But the wind dies out as do old curses.
May these lines stand like the north mountain
As I am like the wolf cub that nurses
At the river's teat, at such a fountain

That we two shall not die but in my word-play
Shall be ever young, light, and stay that way.

Portrait of the Artist as a Young Child

She kept the lamp on late,
floral notebook on her desk
and the sins of the she-wolf:
fraud and betrayal.
Her mother chased her with a knife.
Red devils in her nightmares.

Trailing clouds of glory
at seven she wrote her first
poem about a robin.
What do you want to be
when you grow up?
her aunt, the artist, asked.
A poet, she said.

Her mother sang loudly
and off-key, neither
picked up a pen
nor sat at a typewriter.
The New Yorker lay
about on the coffee table.
> *What if I call*
> *It is not me will it stop*
> *Going Home*
> *I know the bottom*

When she boiled over
among autumnal colors,
her mother didn't
believe her. She said
red and orange rhyme.
You mean they match?
No, she heard

them rhyming
in the lantana
by the pigeon coop.

She learned to name
purple martins and dianthus,
portulaca and mockingbird,
where the ruby-throated
hummingbird oscillates
around the Turk's cap,
and mixed up
the tenses in her poems.
No one taught her any better.
That was the riddle.

Her mother never learned
the names of any flowers
except those for the dead,
marigolds, and the hackberry
tree, which flowers white
in spring and then
turns out the scarlet
berries she thought
were poisonous
by autumn.

Rainy Morning, Early Fall

Hear the Grito of thunder before the mayor of Juárez
gets up this morning for he was awake at midnight,
ringing the bell and shouting it out. Father Miguel,
they hear you still and imitate your call to arms.

Every September around this time, I listen
for the black-chinned hummingbirds,
clattering in the pine and cedar. They're not off
yet for the high plateau of the revolution
in México where I see them in their winter home.

The white statue of Ignacio Allende
stares down at the jardín in San Miguel.
Within hours of the first Grito,
an army of the poor had assembled
and begun to march to México City,
through Atotonilco, the banner of la Virgen
in her starry blue cape held aloft
as they thronged around her.

I hear the birds thrumming overhead,
diving for a sip of the red plastic flower.
Will they leave when the wind blows south
for the geraniums still in bloom
five thousand miles from here?

Allende hung back.
He and Father Miguel were captured and murdered;
the rag-tag army melted back into their impoverished lives.

The hummingbird migrates alone, never in flocks.
Battles for insects and flowers along the route.
All summer the black-chins have fought and mated,

their young have fledged. What is it that calls them to migrate?
A certain slant of light? The cooler mornings?

What calls men to move? A priest in a pulpit,
a general in a nearby colonial city?
Today, on Avenida Dieciséis de Septiembre
people will move in a parade and celebrate
as if there's no migration out of this murderous city
terrorized by drug gangs. The rich migrate to El Paso,
protected by a border. ¿Los pobres? Downtrodden still, again.

Blood Moon

Sleepless at 4:51 am
Mountain Time
when the sandy clouds
cover the eclipse,
a mathematical darkening
of the quantum reservoir
which cannot quite
be snuffed out
like a candle,
I stay in bed
while a world darkens
and the mountains on
the moon gain clarity
in the moment the temperature
ceases to sizzle.
Time for lying awake
in the darkness of
the blood moon,
rising over the mountain
whose time is like no other,
who is thought to hold
a mother or an old man
unlike the one in the moon.
This October moon which I do
not rise and see
under eclipse in the west
on mountain time
covered by clouds
from Hurricane Simon off
the coast of Baja California
where it's Pacific Time,
and El Niño hits San Lucas
hard and again.

The darkness the relief
from sun would bring,
reliefs of mountains and valleys
to the moon's feminine face
double-covered by the clouds
thin and high, not speaking of rain
in the Mountain Time Zone.

Miracle Child

I.
You weren't born in a stable
but a country hospital
in middle-of-nowhere New Mexico
near the Texas state line in oil country.
The wise men of Midland were busy
bringing a diamond drill bit
to dig out a toddler caught in an old well,
covered in caliche concrete, hard stuff,
a different kind of birth than yours
which was filled with florescent light
and your pink skin which rated
a ten on the Apgar scale.
You didn't cry. You looked around,
your brow furrowed, your body
covered in my blood
till nurses wiped and wrapped you.
You fought your way out,
so I never learned to swaddle you
as you seemed tired of confinement,
not comforted by it.
Your father saw you
crown, a gift he has not forgotten.

II.
I do not know how the stars
aligned that October Friday at 10:21 am
except that the sun was in Libra.
I once told you that you were accidental,
not knowing how it would hurt you.
A happy accident, I said.
The happiest. Unplanned, but nothing

was done to prevent your happenstance.
I always felt you chose us for your parents.
I never thought your birth was random chance.

III.
That baby falling into the narrow well
in Midland—now that was an accident.
Baby Jessica, a toddler, her parents
no more than teenagers. I bet she
was unplanned. Chance is fickle:
the orange Monopoly cards
are not always a good thing.
Sometimes you have to pay.
We weren't gambling, but we were
trusting our luck. We were waiting
for you to become in the universe.
We caused the equation to start rumbling
toward its destination, your fortune.
Funny how you have been fascinated
by flipping coins and turning cards,
your misplaced spirituality.

Don't you know
by what you were beckoned,
that by destiny, not accident,
your happy design came to be?
That night-time befalling
when two doors open.
That time you took a fall
into a narrow well
and waited.

Hill Country Blues

On a cloudy day, the sunlight has dripped
into the yellow gallardia and lemon mint.
Wind ruffles the dying live oaks
this autumn, a season of slow death,
as fallen branches morph into serpents.
My father there on the sad heights
of his old age, ravaged body and soul
by Lewy body dementia: white globs
in his brain matter rob him of his dignity.
It is November, the heat is gone, but
the sumac and maple have not yet turned,
and I don't know that he will
last through the soft winter.
Sun slants through clouds.
Then, they cover the sky again.
Such a ray this morning,
that it is not dark, only cloudy.
Brown-eyed Susans nod in the wind,
how short is their season,
combining the light and the dark?

Epiphany, San Miguel

We missed the parade, the Three Kings
riding in on horseback, but not
the polite or sated children
in a line that bent around El Jardín.
Muffled in pink puffy coats, blue hats,
yellow scarves, and fleecy tights,
they huddled against their exhausted
parents who wore that look
of tight-lipped, thinned patience
that comes with the holidays.
This morning the children received
their presents, presented in their shoes
and brought by the Three Kings,
for this is the 12th day of Christmas.

The brass band walks away,
their instruments dented and unpolished,
the silver tuba almost grey,
the only dull spot in the crowd.
The Three Kings sit by the parroquia
while the mayor jokes at the microphone.
These pobrecitos y sus padres
want the photos to begin.
Each child will sit
in the lap of a king and say
thank you for the gifts,
gracias por los regalos.
And the kings will say,
Child, you are a miracle.
Niño, eres milagro.

Wintry Mix in the Chihuahuan Desert

No one predicted a noon wind chill
of 19 degrees, fog, and snow showers.
Even now on television, the forecasters
admit their models don't show it
while I hear snow crunch
against the window pane like sand
swung by a dustdevil in the spring.
All day I have watched it pile up
around the palm tree and on its fronds,
a witness to the snow-tipped pines,
to the vanished Sierra de los Mansos,
socked in by desert snow. The models
say it will end in seven minutes at 1 pm,
but I don't believe it for one minute.
I believe that visibility is down
to one mile, that wind gusts are up
to 35 mph. I am going to drive
the Subaru and wear my snow boots.
Then snuggle up and do sudoku.
Except that the shepherd dog
wants his walk even though snow slants
like flecks of white paint artists dab
in the eyes of portraits, the light
on this fog-bound day, snowing
in the freezing Chihuahuan desert.

Freezing Fog in the El Paso Desert

The fog that crystals on my face as we walk
in the morning weather hides the road,
the fog that knocks on the window pane
in the gray veil of a wizard who doesn't
know which riddle to ask, the fog that grows
during the night like a mushroom, the fog
that descends, fully formed but diaphanous,
yet substantive enough to make the mountains
disappear, closes Transmountain Road.
I ask the fog the oldest riddle I know:
what is it to see and what is it not to see?
I see what hides everything.

Trip Back to Austin

Driving through Dripping Springs
on the way to Resistencia Bookstore
in east Austin, my memory becomes
a book of luminous landmarks,
these limestone cliffs topped by cedar,
my old stomping grounds.
Signs all around me.
Evenings at Lake Travis
with their bursting aorta sunsets
replace visions of Highway 290.
The wind-rippled water, the smoke
clinging to the faces of my friends.
When I see the skyline—
the UT tower, the Capitol dome—
needle leaves settle in
the sharp intake of my breath.
The clouds gather and disperse.
We go down Guadalupe St.—
the Drag—and pass Dobie Mall
and the Harry Ransom Center
where I spent pleasant hours
with a pencil, reading T. S. Eliot
and other 20th century luminaries.
Goodall-Wooten, the frat boy dorm,
is still there but no bookstore,
Garner & Smith's, nor crazy Martha Lee
nor Professor Mackey wandering in
to talk the latest in deconstruction theory—
he's dead now—nor Professor Middleton
getting an espresso in Captain Quackenbush's
café. He's in his eighties, still
writing and publishing poems and essays.

How long ago all this was—
thirty years. Still, so fresh,
this pain of homecoming.
Nostalgia in Greek or *hiearath* in Welsh.
It hits me, they were my age now,
when they mentored me.
At The Mediterranean Café,
I ate Greek salad,
the nephews spaghetti,
my sister, the lamb.
I hear my sister say,
This is where your aunt went to college.
Yes, my alma mater, mother of my soul.

Ode to the Orange

When my fingernail pierces your rind,
a fine spray goldens the air.
Your wrinkled skin doesn't
come off clean,
you, womb of many parts
and few seeds.
When my teeth
break into
your secret pulps,
you spill your juice,
juices no longer at work in me
inside my thin, delicate membranes,
about to break open.

Sitting for the Portrait

Sit still, pick a spot to focus on,
don't look at me, the artist said.
A roomful of people watch
the artist painting me.
Comments. I laugh.
Quit moving, Robin.
I lose my focus on the wall.
So hard to sit perfectly
still. I could not hold
a smile, so I sat for
35 minutes, my lips wistfully
parted. I see that he looks
at me again and again, taking
my measure with his brush.
But what he paints
is all sharp angles.
I look like a strawberry-blonde witch.
He got the hair all right,
but not the eyes or lips.
He paints green irises
without the orange highlights
within or blue ring around them.
Such an intimate act, this close
looking. Being observed
so closely made me nervous.
To portray, from Middle French
and Latin, means to draw forth.
What did he elicit from me,
my inner ugly? What to do
when I saw what he had
observed? Laugh or cry?
Twenty people watching me
closely. I had had no idea

how it was going. So, I finally
smiled. When I arrived home,
my husband asked, How did it go?
See what you think, I said,
and unrolled the thing.
My son screamed.
I would like to have liked it
as the artist is the paramour
of a good friend. But,
when she asked if he could
finish working on it, I said,
well, my husband doesn't like it.
He's my primary observer,
his seeing my first concern.
But she wouldn't drop it.
All the more reason for him
to finish it. Oh, it's finished,
I thought as I toted it to the garage,
to un-see the seeing of what
this not-so-great artist had seen.

Small Pools in a Dry Río Grande

The Great Blue Heron stays by the empty river
while the Divine explodes in every star.
A few minnows angle in pools left over from drought
as Divinity suffers. A father and son also fish
for the rare minnows to use as bait at the big lake
north of here, Elephant Butte. I try to figure out
how Divinity suffers while the dog bites the heads
off dead fish and romps through the small pools.
Four and a half billion years after a super-nova
rocked a cloud of dust and gas,
the heron nests in Afghan pines on the east bank.
An underground channel keeps the river alive
while the barest spark hints at the Divinity.
Some activists filed suit on behalf of the river.
The heron reflects by the small pools and considers
dancing as I wonder why no one sued in her name.
I follow heron footprints in dry sand, so much sand
in my shoes, it bruises my toes. The dog splashes
in small pools, and the heron flies off to her nest.
In slow wingbeats, I hear the Divine Rhythm.
Observed and unobserved, supernovae burst around us.
The pine trembles as she settles on a large branch,
scaly feet around it, midnight wings folding.

The Future

Time is a fundamental,
asymmetrical force.
As soon as we are grounded
in the elements, we realize
to age and die is erasure
of dear faces. The stars
will grow pale and ashen,
no more to explode
and litter spacetime
with carbon, oxygen,
and iron. Do we ride
on the boom of a black
hole sailing in time
like the one in
the middle of our galaxy?
The streaming light
is information,
and when it goes
out, it's gone as it thunders
through the night.
It's gone, same as a photograph,
created in a darkroom,
my grandmother had
on her wall of a bride
on the steps and the verse
inscribed below
vanished as well except
phrases echoing,
one line missing:

"Until heaven and earth shall pass away,
Until the stars grow cold and dim,
/… /
She hath plighted her love to him."
I didn't know what it meant then.
Now, I do. I have sworn it,
the future I mean with you.

Poem

I thought of an idea
nestled in a meridian-blue egg
but it did not hatch
into a poem.
Instead, it was a homely,
hungry creature with raw skin
so delicate it could not
be touched early on.
Then, prickly quills grew
quickly. I fed it
the range of the 12 senses,
the small dog skull
we found at the park,
the cloudless day,
and the wind last night
which roughed up
the pines until at last
feathers grew in
over a few weeks,
and the idea fledged
and launched itself.
I followed it till it was
out of eye and earshot.
So, I am left
with a tree, a cottonwood,
whose leaves will soon
be yellow, whose branches
harbor more nests.

Signs of the Times

The white buffalo has been born
in the west and the two-headed calf.

      How can you be sure these are the signs?

An unkindness of white ravens
rises in the northwestern forests.

      Did you note the eclipse of the Harvest Moon?
      Have you thought long about the sunset?

      Well, have you?

A pink dolphin frolics in a Louisiana lake.

      What does it all mean?

      Have you studied the names and added
      their numbers, analyzed the qualities
      of heat and moisture, cold and dryness?

      What does it mean to be here in this world
      of physical properties where lead doesn't
      transmute to gold, but poisons the water?

Rattlesnakes coil in limestone cliffs
strung with opal gemstones: creatures of fire.

The soft blue damselflies, born of water,
hover so near, I could write with one,
their ink of the sky.

Where is the modern elixir, our hunting
of the green lion and the yellow lodestone?

While children are caged beside a fictional border.
Where the mercury thermometer rages upward,
and the coyote breathes in smoke-filled air.

The Garden of Hope

Sunlight on creosote in early fall,
season of jeweled dragonflies like fallen sky
and butterflies—sulfur, blue, and white—
desert petrichor after a short, plunging rain,
brilliant coyote scat on the trail, hearing him
blurt in the daylight arroyo behind ballfields
while men stand in wonder on the dam,
as my dog and I pass close on the side.

Season's change, though this is the one
when the dark comes earlier and stays
later; still, I have hope when I hear
you get up without groaning, hope
that one day you'll walk freely again.
I hope winter snow won't break branches
off the acacia or desert willow, that it will freeze
seeds that need it and ready them.
I hope to grow chocolate daisies in spring,
but for fall, I put in the crops of garlic
and cilantro, red kale, and rainbow chard.

At a Trumpet's Blast

We shall become known
whereas until that time we shall have been
unknown to ourselves, such as dark matter
is known by absence of light and presence
of gravity, starlight leaking.
If this absence of photons is your answer.
Whatever the question was, it's the one
you've been given. Let go your cupped hands
so that the solitary leaf-cutter bee can pollinate
the star-crossed bougainvillea and solar flare tecoma.
She is all the universe we'll ever need,
dark matter nesting in the knotty pine fence.
Her monotonous song, ever-circling.
When the trumpet sounds, will we be
left behind? Will she be the one transformed?
Say it to the scrub desert, your answer
is the pollen, golden sacrament on black
legs, this galaxy now, circling a black hole
and whatever dark matter holds it all together.

This Grace

Sunshimmer on creosote
shifts from yellow
blossom to furry grey seed.
     And I have seen this happen.
Yellow-eyed hawk looking
into my green eyes:
     the startle of it, the flash
     of gratitude and danger
I had for being there by the arroyo.
When the coyote snarled, I stood
     there stupefied with grace.
The dog immobile in hot May sun.

We moved on, impelled
by what we cannot name.

As if the word coyote
or falcon would be something.

And words, listen,
there's a singer in the park, uttering prayer
in a language strange to me.

A yellow songbird,
the western meadowlark,
lifts into the blue
from the old acacia stand,
lighting there again and
rattling unfallen seed.

All the Time in the World

There was no clock in the studio
with northern light
at the big house in Wichita Falls.
Aunt Mary's face and fingers
smudged with oil paint,
she didn't keep track of the time
it took her to paint
portraits of the ones she loved
except for her squirming son,
who wouldn't sit still
for the time she needed.
She came back inside time
for him and his sister
and the husband she adored.

I live without alarm clocks.
Time stretches when I write.
At least I can tell night from day.
Aunt Mary sometimes could not.
How she painted that mesquite tree
in the wind, branches thrashing,
time and time again.

El Paso Artist Hal Marcus Starts with the Frame

A great black frame requires
this Black Madonna who tilts her head
at extreme angles, something odd
about her eyeballs, what enthralls me
I cannot say: the stars on her azure cape,
the triangle above her head, golden,
pinks and blues and maybes,
just a thought behind the veil,
finished and signed this morning
with a handful of glitter, a palette
of color to be tasted
like berry marmalade,
her glory of fruit plucked out
of the cosmos of nuns and angels,
her light in jeweled paint
Hal plucked out of the cosmos
just now and started with the frame;
then this white frame for the blue ink,
her head at an extreme angle
as she eyes me full of grammar
and the glamour of pomegranate trees
while the ground too is jeweled here,
and the yellow jacket as well, mad
jewel plucked out of the cosmos.

Morning Mosaic

in Hal Marcus' garden

White birds against North Mountain
     bounce out of the wetlands.
Coyote crosses the trail in sunlight
     out of his midnight den.
A waning gibbous moon lights up
     creosote and leafless lacy mesquite.
Desert marigold long since dormant.

Every staircase is a marvel.
     One saint has a pet iguana.
San Miguel defeats ignorance by his sword.
     The Hermit carries his own light.

Above the lilies, Frida Kahlo's face in tin.

How to Catch a Hummingbird

Consider that you too
are a being made of light
but also a benevolent giant.

In the big mulberry
a nest has come to be,
and you walk right up
to touch a fledgling,
the mother bird fiercely
chattering in your face.

After a violent July thunderstorm
when the lightning stops striking,
you pick the nestling up off the ground
and put it back, but overnight
the naked pink thing wiggles out
of the destroyed nest,
which you then repair with adhesive tape,
and put the nestling back again,
and this time, the mother doesn't mind.

Otherwise, you leave them alone
and train a prismatic telescope on the nest,
on her translucent yellow straw
of a tongue, feeding the young.

You catch him fledging,
he's falling, he catches himself up,
and he's rainbow, rainbow, rainbow.

Amending the Soil

I plant thorny acacia on purpose
where western sun blasts the brick wall.
Rose grows wild with orange rosehips
I gather for a tea rich in vitamin C.
It doesn't rain in the spring,
and jackrabbits come where the acacia
has grown bitter roots. Coyotes follow.
Thick dust rolls in, red clouds of it.
Blooms of desert marigold but only deathly
datura gives off warped and beautiful visions.
My arms scratched, I bleed onto the sandy soil.
And it doesn't make any difference.
What grows there protects itself
and blooms where it wants.

Riddle

Her blue shadow as four sisters flee
daylight to hide behind the megaliths
flattens out to squeeze through
tighter than a pencil skirt
no room left to skirt through
the granite shale.

The rabbit moon is new and slender
like the daggers she keeps in her red cave.
Grey hair and fur in her scat;
the hare goddess defeated again
leaping for her life
turning the wrong way.

Into the darkness best left to darkness
as her shadow comes with her inside,
not disappeared by dawnlight.
In the arroyo, she has staked her claim.
Her time isn't long.
She's been hungry.

ACKNOWLEDGMENTS

"August Rain Melancholia," *Texas Weather Anthology*, Lamar University Literary Press, 2016.

"Ode to the Apple," 2nd place, Wilda Morris' Poetry Challenge, February 2017.

"Hill Country Blues," *Ponder Review,* Spring 2019.

"This Grace," *Gyroscope Review*, Spring 2019.

"At Faywood Hot Springs, New Mexico," *Pilgrimage*, Vol. 44, Spring 2019.

"Poem," *The Main Street Rag*, Spring 2020.

"Signs of the Times," "Small Pools in a Dry Rio Grande," and "At a Trumpet's Blast;" *Hole in the Head Review*, Summer, 2021.

"Ridge of High Pressure," *Cutthroat Literary Review,* Summer 2022.

"To My Husband as I Near My 54th Birthday," *The Ocotillo Review*, Spring 2022.

"The Garden of Hope," *Pilgrimage*, 2022.

AUTHOR'S BIOGRAPHY

A native of Austin, Texas, who grew up just north of Dallas, Robin Scofield is the author of *Flow*, named Southwest Book of the Year in 2019, and *Sunflower Cantos*, from Mouthfeel Press. Scofield graduated from the University of Texas at Austin with a B.A. in English and an M.A. in Creative Writing where she received the Christopher Morley Poetry Prize, and studied with Albert Goldbarth, David Wevill, and Richard Howard. She put down roots in El Paso 30 years ago and worked the academic fields as a migrant scholar, teaching everything from basic writing to Rhetoric of the Holocaust. She has been published in *The Paris Review, Western Humanities Review, The Texas Observer, About Place Journal, Pilgrimage, Theology Today, The Texas Poetry Calendar, The San Pedro River Review, Cimarron Review, descant, The Ocotillo Review, and The Rio Grande Review*. She writes with the Tumblewords Project in El Paso, Texas, where she lives with her husband.

www.ingramcontent.com/pod-product-compliance
Lightning Source LLC
Chambersburg PA
CBHW051643120626
46551CB00015B/2198